Roots English

Book 1

Big Max

Frog & Toad

Golly Sisters Go West

Emma's Strange Pet

Toem Books

John Stephen Knodell

ISBN – 978-4-908152-16-0

Toem Books, Minami 9, 1-16, Chuo ku,

Sapporo, Japan 0640809

Dedicated to

Hana

How to Use the Book

The Roots English series is a content-based textbook that uses authentic readings with grammar, writing, and speaking exercises. While the textbook is rich with grammar exercises, exercises can be used to A) create conversations from the grammar exercises B) test students on the problematic grammar points throughout the book, and C) connect the reading book with sections of the textbook, for example, the making perfect sentences and grammar focus sections.

For classes studying English approximately 3-4 hours a week, try to finish one reading section, one grammar focus/preposition/article exercise, and one writing assignment. Each week, test students on one of the grammar exercises, have a review test of the vocabulary, and always use the textbook as an opportunity to speak with students.

About the Author

John Stephen Knodell has an M.Ed. in TESOL, and has been an English language teacher for over 20 years. He has taught students from 2 years old to students over 80, from private classes to classes of over 100 students. He currently teaches at a university in Japan.

Table of Contents

Reading Section

Part 1

VOCABULARY TO LEARN

detective, everyone, stolen, jumbo, umbrella, took a deep breath, blew, south,

missing, burning

QUESTIONS

1. What was Max's job?

2. What did the king lose?

3. How did Max go to the king?

4. Can birds smell?

Part 2

VOCABULARY TO LEARN

ship, captain, burning, smoke, pocket, pipe, forgot, travel, waiting

QUESTIONS

1. How did Max go to the ship?

2. What was burning?

3. Where was the Captain's pipe?

4. Why is it good to have an umbrella?

5. Was the king waiting for Max?

Part 3

VOCABULARY TO LEARN

led, showed him, not that much, palace, full of, charge a lot, steal, sad

QUESTIONS

1. Where did the king lead Max?

2. What color are emeralds?

3. Does Max charge a lot of money?

4. How old is Jumbo?

5. How did Jumbo feel in the palace?

Part 4

VOCABULARY TO LEARN

led, a lock, gate, courtyard, high walls, climb, the only key, stolen, footprints,

except, wet, perhaps

QUESTIONS

1. Where did the king last see Jumbo?

2. What can't elephants climb?

3. How many keys are there for the lock?

4. Does it always rain in Pooka Pooka?

Part 5

Vocabulary to Learn

wonderful, little pieces, melts, wall, hill, tracks, follow

Questions

1. How was the weather?

2. What does the ice do very fast?

3. What was on the other side of the wall?

4. Did Max and the king walk slowly down the hill?

Part 6

Vocabulary to Learn

tears, clue, secret, followed, trail, suddenly, loud, sound

Questions

1. What was the clue?

2. Did the king know why Jumbo was unhappy?

3. What sound did they hear?

4. Was the sound from an elephant?

Part 7

VOCABULARY TO LEARN

tears, crocodile, path, sharp, tongue, bite, I take your word for itpushed,

nearly, fooled me, jungle

QUESTIONS

1. What kind of tongue does a crocodile have?

2. What is bigger, an elephant's or crocodile's tears?

3. Why can't the crocodile bite Max?

4. Why did the crocodile cry?

5. Where did Max and the king go next?

Part 8

VOCABULARY TO LEARN

shook, earthquake, pointed, solved, followed, trail, steps, fooled me

QUESTIONS

1. What made the ground shake?

2. What kind of party did the elephants have?

3. Could Jumbo talk?

4. How did Jumbo go over the wall?

The End

VOCABULARY TO LEARN

the top of, high, important, especially, invite, palace, treasures, reward, if you

don't mind, would rather, took a deep breath

QUESTIONS

1. Are birthday parties important to elephants?

2. Where will the birthday party be next year?

3. What did Max want to eat?

4. What did Big Max blow into?

5. Did you like this story?

Chapter 1

VOCABULARY TO LEARN

knocked, wonderful, brought, wear, pushed, scarf, trying to kill me, tramped,

sled, behind

QUESTIONS

1. What season is it in the story?

2. What doesn't Toad have?

3. What did Frog bring for Toad?

4. What did they do outside?

5. Does Toad like winter?

VOCABULARY TO LEARN

a bump, rushed past, leaped over, steer, crow, nearby, alone, dived

QUESTIONS

1. How did Frog fall off the sled?

2. What does it mean STEER?   a) fall   b) drive   c) bounce   d) fly

3. What did the crow tell Toad?

4. What happened to Toad?

5. What does Toad think is better than winter?

Chapter 2

VOCABULARY TO LEARN

caught in the rain, wet, spoiled, near, stove, dry, pollywog, spring, around the

corner, pebbles, meadow, worm, tree stump

QUESTIONS

1. How was the weather?

2. How can clothes dry fast?

3. What does it mean "Just around the corner"? a) it is very hot   b) it is very far   c) it is very soon   d) it is very cold

4. What did Frog find in the woods?

5. What did Frog find in the meadow?

VOCABULARY TO LEARN

corner, spring, river, mud, lizard, chasing his tail, garden, found it, hurried

QUESTIONS

1.   What did Frog find around the corner of the river?

2.   How was the weather?

3.   After the river, where did Frog go?

4.   What were his mom and dad doing?

5.   After it stopped raining, where did Frog and Toad go?

Chapter 3

VOCABULARY TO LEARN

pond, I wish, sweet, I'll be back soon, bought, licked, drops, melting, dripped,

splattered

QUESTIONS

1. What did Frog want to eat?

2. What kind of ice cream did they like?

3. What happened to the ice cream?

4. Where did the ice cream fall?

5. What couldn't Toad do because of the ice cream?

VOCABULARY TO LEARN

pond, mouse, awful, covered, sticks, leaves, horns, hid, good heavens, sank,

never mind, shade

QUESTIONS

1. Where was Frog waiting for Toad?

2. What did the rabbit say was on Toad's head?

3. Where did Frog hide?

4. Did Toad jump into the pond?

5. Could Frog and Toad eat ice cream?

Chapter 4

Vocabulary to Learn

leaves, fallen off, on the ground, rake, lawn, garden shed, ran through the

woods, guess

Questions

1. Where were the leaves?

2. What did Frog and Toad want to do with the leaves?

3. Where was Toad's rake?

4. How did Frog go to Toad's house?

5. Was Frog at home when Toad went there?

VOCABULARY TO LEARN

raked, leaves, a pile, lawn, soon, wind, blew, everywhere, clean up, get to

work

QUESTIONS

1. Where did Frog put the leaves? a) into a pond   b) into a group   c) into a fire   d) into his house

2. After Toad finished raking, where did he go?

3. Why did the leaves go everywhere?

4. When will Frog and Toad clean up their leaves?

5. Why were Frog and Toad happy at night?

Chapter 5

VOCABULARY TO LEARN

decorated, broken, worried, deep hole, path, lost, woods, wet, chased, cellar,

lantern

QUESTIONS

1.   What season is it in the story now?

2.   What is broken in the story?

3.   Why was Toad worried?

4.   Where does Toad think Frog is lost?

5.   What kind of animal might be chasing Frog?

The End

REVIEW VOCABULARY FROM BOOK

Chased, a pile, wet, cellar, blew, pebbles, lantern, wonderful, shade, lawn,

rake, horns, stove, behind, never mind

QUESTIONS

1. What will Toad hit with a pan?

2. Why was Frog late?

3. How many questions did Toad ask Frog?

4. How did Frog get to Toad's home?

5. What did you think about the story?

Chapter 1

VOCABULARY TO LEARN

sat, wagon, west, makes me mad, something is wrong with, walked around,

giddy up

QUESTIONS

1. Where were the Golly sisters going?

2. Why were they mad?

3. What is the horse word for GO?

4. Who is stronger, May-May or the horse?

VOCABULARY TO LEARN

stop, got into, wagon, took, reins, we are on our way

QUESTIONS

1. Who said STOP?

2. What is the horse word for stop?

3. What do reins do?   A) Hurt the horse   B) Drive the horse   C) Massage the horse   D) Keep the horse warm

4. Why do they want to go west?

Chapter 2

VOCABULARY TO LEARN

peeped, curtain, go first, you look funny, everybody, admit it, together

QUESTIONS

1. Why did the sisters fight?   a) because of the dress   b) because of going first   c) because of the dogs

2. What does it mean, 'Look funny'?   a) look strange   b) look happy   c) look angry

3. Did they both go first?

4. Where did the people go?

5. Who watched the show?

Chapter 3

VOCABULARY TO LEARN

lost, afraid, worried, make tea, first, second, third, fourth, together, check,

clapping, in the middle of, bowed

QUESTIONS

1. Was May-May worried about being lost?

2. What is the third thing they do when they are lost?

3. What song did Rose sing?

4. What did they hear outside the wagon?

5. Did they give a terrible show?

Chapter 4

VOCABULARY TO LEARN

want, the show, remember, trust me, do the rest, ready, did not move

QUESTIONS

1. What does May-May want?

2. Does Rose think the horse can dance?

3. Who got on the horse that night?

4. Did the horse move?

VOCABULARY TO LEARN

while, waiting, heard, giddy-up, moved, jumped, stage, through, out of the

town, late

QUESTIONS

1. What did Rose do while waiting for May-May?

2. What did the horse do when May-May said 'Giddy-up'?

3. Where did the horse go?

4. When did May-May come back?

Chapter 5

VOCABULARY TO LEARN

loses, are you ready, pretty, cannot find, makes me mad, my turn, yelled, hide,

no harm has been done

QUESTIONS

1. What can't May-May find?

2. What kind of hat does she have?

3. What did May-May do while Rose was singing?

4. Where was the hat?

5. Do you think Rose hid May-May's hat?

VOCABULARY TO LEARN

yelled, squashing, could not find, sad, began, clap, forgive

QUESTIONS

1. What did May-May want to do first?

2. What happened to Rose's hair?

3. What kind of dance did May-May do?

4. How do you know the people liked the dance?

5. Was May-May still angry with her sister?

Chapter 6

VOCABULARY TO LEARN

dark, moon, outside, why should I, hear, sat up, remember, look funny, fuss,

did not let me finish, stars shone

QUESTIONS

1. Could the Golly Sisters see the moon?

2. Why were they afraid?

3. Who went outside?

4. What does FUSS mean?   a) talk   b) fight   c) sing   d) monkey

5. Do the Golly Sisters like each other?

Chapter 1

VOCABULARY TO LEARN

fetch, look up, make her _____, sneeze, shouted, across from, all mine,

allergic to, wheeze, eyes sore

QUESTIONS

1. Who is the owner of Lucky?

2. What does Max want?

3. Where was Sally reading her book?

4. Why can't Max get a dog?

5. What was Emma eating for dinner?

VOCABULARY TO LEARN

furry, give up, how about, not fair, strange, it's hard for, rabbit, jumped up

QUESTIONS

1.   What kind of pets can't they have?

2.   What kinds of pets does Max want, except dogs?

3.   What kinds of pets don't have fur?

4.   Does Emma want a bicycle for her birthday?

5.   When is Emma's birthday?

Chapter 2

VOCABULARY TO LEARN

birthday, ate fast, shouted, mice, hamsters, lizard, hole, tiny, misses his friend

QUESTIONS

1. How did Max and Emma eat?

2. What is the name of the pet store?

3. What kinds of animals were in the store?

4. Was the lizard big or small?

5. How many lizards were in the store, 1 or 2?

VOCABULARY TO LEARN

stranger, softly, jumped up and down, crickets, feed, mom made a face,

from...to..., fish tank

QUESTIONS

1.   What was the lizard's name?

2.   What colors could the lizard change into?

3.   What kind of food did the lizard eat?

4.   Why did the mom make a face?

5.   Where did the storeowner put the lizard?

Chapter 3

VOCABULARY TO LEARN

furry, sand, flat, piece of wood, a hole, hide, peek out, a dish, for ages, shot ,

across, he's sweet

QUESTIONS

1. What did Emma put in the tank?

2. What color did the lizard turn into?

3. How long did it take the lizard to change colors?

4. Did the lizard walk slowly across the tank?

5. Where did the lizard hide?

VOCABULARY TO LEARN

I guess so, strange, reach, poke, feed, tweezers, cricket, wiggled, shot around,

snapped up

QUESTIONS

1. What did Emma tell Max not to do?

2. How did Emma feed Stranger?

3. How many crickets did Stranger eat?

4. Did Stranger eat the cricket slowly?

5. How many crickets can you eat?

Chapter 4

VOCABULARY TO LEARN

snapped up, sat still, fed, no way, sad, dish, might, stared

QUESTIONS

1. Where did Stranger drink water from?

2. Is Stranger happy now?

3. Where did Josh want to put Stranger?

4. What color did Josh think Stranger could be?

5. Did Emma want Josh to put Stranger on his shirt?

VOCABULARY TO LEARN

adopted, sort of, new, belong here, at last, glad, worm

QUESTIONS

1. Who is Stranger like?

2. Does Emma want her brother to be an anole?

3. Why doesn't Emma want her brother to be a lizard?

4. What do anoles eat?

5. Do you think Max likes his home?

Chapter 5

VOCABULARY TO LEARN

look for, behind, sure, shouted, hiding, hit, look around, couldn't stand it,

grabbed

QUESTIONS

1. Where did Emma look for Stranger?

2. How did Emma know Max did something bad?

3. How old is Max?

4. What did Emma want to do to Max??

5. If Max didn't tell Emma where Stranger was, who would she tell?

VOCABULARY TO LEARN

peeping out, on top of, hiding, hair, furry, mine, I wish, lizards, far away

QUESTIONS

1. Where was Stranger?

2. Why did Emma laugh?

3. What kind of pets does Max like?

4. When is Max's birthday?

5. Why is Max sad?

Chapter 6

VOCABULARY TO LEARN

tank, needs, far away, too, only, a box, another, this is for you, strange, wizard

QUESTIONS

1. What does Stranger need?

2. Where does Stranger live?

3. What was inside the box?

4. Did Max want the anole?

5. How do we know Max was happy?

VOCABULARY TO LEARN

ran, put, watched, shot, behind, peeked out, get along

QUESTIONS

1. How did Max go to Stranger's tank?

2. Where did Wizard hide?

3. Do Max and Emma get along?

4. How many lizards do you have in your home?

5. If you were a lizard, what would you eat

Grammar
Focus Section

Grammar Focus 1

*All of the sentences below have mistakes. You must correct the sentences, and make them **PERFECT**.*

1. I have pen, apple, and dog in my bag.

2. This books is good.

3. I eating pizza right now.

4. Tomorrow, I go school.

5. Every day, I am watch the TV.

6. My sister bed is big.

7. I have not a computer.

8. A elephant is big than a cat.

9. He is tallest boy in mine class.

10. Can I having a glass of water?

Grammar Focus 2

All of the sentences below have mistakes. You must correct the sentences, and make them **PERFECT**.

1. In morning, I drink glass of water.

2. I study always before tests.

3. Yesterday, I sleep early.

4. It is raining because I have my umbrella.

5. He like chocolate and he doesn't like cake.

6. My dog is a small.

7. There is sunny today.

8. It is a book on the table.

9. At Saturday, I usually wake up late.

10. I go to a school on bus.

Grammar Focus 3

1. She is good on tennis.

2. I am wanting to play the tennis.

3. I live in 3rd floor.

4. What do you like color?

5. What kind sport you like?

6. I like dog.

7. She will buys a new car.

8. The next week, they visit Tokyo.

9. He study hard, but his teacher is happy.

10. If it rain tomorrow, I wear rainboots.

Grammar Focus 4

All of the sentences below have mistakes. You must correct the sentences, and make them **PERFECT**.

1. I got today up 7am.

2. It cool outside.

3. It maybe will rainy today.

4. I can't finding book.

5. I am thinking you are a smart.

6. Yesterday, I take a trip in Tokyo.

7. Can you tell to me you name?

8. I work to 10am from 5pm.

9. I will call to you tomorrow's night.

10. The baby monkey try to climb tree.

Grammar Focus 5

1. How many of pencils does you have?

2. I am drink water right now.

3. Every morning, I play piano.

4. I am needing to call to my mom. It's her birthday.

5. I sad because I lost my a socks.

6. My eyes color are brown.

7. Our class begin on 4pm.

8. He talk slow.

9. She walk fastly.

10. I singing nice.

Grammar Focus 6

All of the sentences below have mistakes. You must correct the sentences, and make them **PERFECT**.

1. I can't hear radio. Please turn it down.

2. Please write you name in this paper.

3. Please sit down the chair.

4. Please standing up.

5. Who did you met 2 day ago?

6. My pen is made by Japan.

7. He shoes is stinky.

8. In night, I always brush my tooth.

9. She have 2 foot.

10. It is 5 man in the car.

Grammar Focus 7

All of the sentences below have mistakes. You must correct the sentences, and make them **PERFECT**.

1. Can I have a water?

2. You should eat a rice every day.

3. He will buy a glove tomorrow.

4. I don't want to eat a chicken for a dinner.

5. There is many of cars in the world.

6. I have few computer.

7. A little people can fly airplanes.

8. How much dictionaries do you having?

9. I don't have some helicopter.

10. This is book are heavy.

Grammar Focus 8

All of the sentences below have mistakes. You must correct the sentences, and make them **PERFECT**.

1. I have angry because my sister hit me leg.

2. She never kind at me.

3. I hope she are nice for me.

4. My mom want her clean her room.

5. I want her to stop to hit me.

6. My dad want me to smart.

7. I study hardly every on Sunday.

8. Sometimes, I am want to go to outside.

9. We went to the Niseko by a car.

10. We went to camping, and it was funny.

Grammar Focus 9

All of the sentences below have mistakes. You must correct the sentences, and make them **PERFECT**.

1. I have a Japan car.

2. My car color is purple color.

3. I like to eat apple red.

4. Let pick apples in the summer.

5. Study English is difficult.

6. Play soccer is funny.

7. Watch movie is interesting.

8. I am interest in game.

9. I would like buy a new game.

10. I have never go to Okinawa.

Grammar Focus 10

All of the sentences below have mistakes. You must correct the sentences, and make them **PERFECT**.

1. Where is your from?

2. Where are you live?

3. How many old are you?

4. How much brother do you have?

5. How you come here today?

6. How often do you watching movie?

7. Does you like study?

8. Can you swimming fastly?

9. What you eat for a dinner yesterday?

10. If it snow tomorrow, what you wear?

Grammar Focus 11

All of the sentences below have mistakes. You must correct the sentences, and make them **PERFECT**.

1. I in the morning ride sometimes my bike.

2. There is sunny today.

3. If I hungry, I eat a bread.

4. It is book on the table.

5. This pants is dirty.

6. I have not a elephant.

7. In night, bird sleep in trees.

8. The cat jumped under the cup.

9. A tiger live on Africa.

10. I want play on the park.

Grammar Focus 12

All of the sentences below have mistakes. You must correct the sentences, and make them **PERFECT**.

1. I am live on 3rd floor.

2. He is a Japanese, nice boy.

3. She have a new, small eraser.

4. They have a plastic, red ball.

5. He paint nice.

6. She dance beautiful.

7. We play game right now.

8. Yesterday, I drink a milk.

9. After this class, I go to home.

10. Car is fast than a dog.

Grammar Focus 13

All of the sentences below have mistakes. You must correct the sentences, and make them **PERFECT**.

1. Russia is big country in the world.

2. I have to must do homework.

3. If I don't homework, my mom angry.

4. I like apple but oranges.

5. It is hot, or I want drink water.

6. She is loudly.

7. They are taking trip in Canada.

8. Please sit the table.

9. My table is made wood.

10. There is a big, brown table.

Grammar Focus 14

All of the sentences below have mistakes. You must correct the sentences, and make them **PERFECT**.

1. Playing sports are funny.

2. Eating pizza and ice cream are yummy.

3. Please stop to talk. You are noise.

4. I woke up 6am today.

5. I wash face before I sleeping.

6. Can you carried my bag? They are heavy.

7. I like don't homework.

8. Every boys is play soccer.

9. In Friday, I will visit to my friend.

10. She is an great dance.

Grammar Focus 15

1. They likes play with toy.

2. Hurry on! You late.

3. I am interesting in writing stories.

4. What kind jam do you liking?

5. All of monkeys eat bananas.

6. Nurse works in hospital.

7. He feet smell like a onion.

8. She looks a nice girl.

9. Don't push to me.

10. This is last sentence. Yahoooooo...

Prepositions Section

Prepositions 1

Fill in the blank
Write a proper preposition for each sentence. Sometimes, there is more than one answer. Also, prepositions are used in Idioms. These phrasal verbs must be memorized.

1. My friend is _____ Brazil.

2. He moved _____ this city last year.

3. He likes everything _____ this city.

4. I think he is happy _____ his new school and friends.

5. It is difficult _____ his mom to speak English.

6. _____ Brazil, people speak Portuguese.

7. I'm not good _____ speaking Portuguese.

8. _____ the future, I want to visit Brazil.

9. I will play soccer _____ a beach.

10. I dream _____ playing soccer _____ people in Brazil.

Prepositions 2

1. We took a trip _____ France. It was fantastic.

2. We went to France _____ airplane.

3. I eat soup _____ a spoon.

4. I sometimes put salt _____ my vegetable soup.

5. After she got home _____ school, she practiced the violin.

6. She is good _____ playing the violin.

7. The violin is made _____ wood.

8. The violin was made _____ Germany.

9. He made some toast _____ breakfast.

10. I drank a glass _____ water.

Prepositions 3

1. I read a book _____ a frog and a toad. It was funny.

2. My mom has to go shopping _____ milk. We don't have any more.

3. I got _____ the bus, and went to school.

4. _____ school, I had a test. It was hard.

5. After school, I had a fight _____ a boy. He's mean.

6. He runs _____ a cheetah. He's so fast.

7. I made 5 mistakes _____ the test. I was happy.

8. My friend made 0 mistakes. She got an A+ _____ the test.

9. She likes to draw pictures _____ birds.

10. I borrowed a book _____ my friend.

Prepositions 4

1. The book is _____ dragons.

2. Can you give a pencil _____ me? I don't have one.

3. What did you do _____ your vacation?

4. Don't forget to bring your lunch _____ you.

5. I bought 2 tickets _____ the movie.

6. My dog catches balls _____ his mouth.

7. I sometimes think _____ playing baseball.

8. She came here _____ her mom. They came together.

9. He does his homework _____ his bed.

10. My grandma eats vegetables _____ her health.

Prepositions 5

1. I got _____ _____ 6am today.

2. My mom puts _____ make-up every morning.

3. I brush my teeth _____ a toothbrush.

4. He is sitting _____ his desk.

5. Please sit _____ and take _____ your coat.

6. I saw a ghost _____ my dream yesterday.

7. The ghost spoke to me _____ Chinese. It was strange.

8. I don't speak Chinese _____ all.

9. So why did I have a dream _____ a Chinese ghost?

10. Tonight, I will sleep _____ my mom and dad.

Prepositions 6

Fill in the blank
Write a proper preposition for each sentence. Sometimes, there is more than one answer. Also, prepositions are used in Idioms. These phrasal verbs must be memorized.

1. Everybody, please stand _____. We are going outside.

2. We are going to play _____ the park.

3. We will play _____ balls and boomerangs and bats.

4. We will go to the park _____ foot.

5. She lives _____ the 7th floor.

6. The view _____ her apartment is beautiful.

7. She lives _____ herself.

8. She was born _____ 1979 _____ a hospital.

9. He wrote a letter _____ his friend.

10. He wrote _____ parks and ghosts and apartments.

Prepositions 7

Fill in the blank
Write a proper preposition for each sentence. Sometimes, there is more than one answer. Also, prepositions are used in Idioms. These phrasal verbs must be memorized.

1.   There is an eraser _____ the floor.

2.   There is some rice _____ your hair. Can I eat it?

3.   The cake is made _____ eggs, erasers, and eggplant. It's delicious.

4.   Yuck. The cake tastes _____ an old shoe.

5.   Let's go swimming. Put _____ your bathing suit.

6.   Be careful when you dive _____ the diving board.

7.   Hurry _____. You are late _____ school.

8.   Let's go. I'll drive you _____ school.

9.   My mom talks _____ the phone a lot.

10. She always talks _____ a long time.

Prepositions 8

1. Maybe she is _____ love _____ the phone.

2. I had a good time _____ the party.

3. I gave a present _____ my friend.

4. She was so happy that she put her arms _____ me. It was a hug.

5. I don't like hugs _____ all.

6. She was very happy _____ the present.

7. Who are you talking _____?

8. We will go home _____ a minute.

9. I clean my home _____ a vacuum.

10. I clean my home _____ 30 minutes everyday.

Prepositions 9

1. I'm interested _____ cleaning.

2. Because if I don't clean, my home looks _____ a jungle.

3. Please listen _____ me.

4. I want you to get _____ _____ this room.

5. He just took _____ his socks.

6. The smell _____ his feet is really, really, really bad.

7. What did you say? I can't hear you. Speak _____.

8. There is snow _____ top _____ Mt. Fuji.

9. It looks _____ a giant ice cream cone.

10. Do you want to eat lunch _____ me?

Prepositions 10

1. We can go _____ a pizza restaurant.

2. Sorry, I can't go. I have no money _____ my pocket.

3. Don't worry. I'll pay _____ you.

4. Your feet are _____ the table.

5. Maybe socks are _____ your feet.

6. Do you wash your feet _____ soap?

7. The apple is hanging _____ the tree.

8. I want to make apple pie _____ the apple.

9. _____ apples, we can't make apple pie.

10. Look _____ the mountain. It's really high.

Prepositions 11

Fill in the blank
Write a proper preposition for each sentence. Sometimes, there is more than one answer. Also, prepositions are used in Idioms. These phrasal verbs must be memorized.

1. I can see people walking _____ the mountain.

2. Oh no. A man is falling _____ the mountain. Ouch!

3. I think his friend will take him _____ a hospital.

4. I want to live _____ a mountain, but not to close.

5. Let's go to sleep. Please turn _____ the lights.

6. A; Which movie do you want to watch?   B: I don't care. It's _____ to you.

7. A: Let's watch Pizzaman. I'm crazy _____ pizza.

8. (After the movie) B: What did you think _____ the movie?

9. So-so. I fell asleep _____ 10 minutes.

10. I have the same jacket _____ you.

Prepositions 12

Fill in the blank
Write a proper preposition for each sentence. Sometimes, there is more than one answer. Also, prepositions are used in Idioms. These phrasal verbs must be memorized.

1. The number 5 is _____ the number 4.

2. Do my shoes smell _____ pizza?

3. She always takes a trip _____ herself.

4. He drinks lots _____ water _____ his health.

5. My nose is _____ my face.

6. My mouth is _____ my nose.

7. My eyes are _____ my nose.

8. Stop putting your finger _____ your nose.

9. Why do you always talk _____ your nose?

10. I would like to live _____ a lake.

Prepositions 13

Fill in the blank
Write a proper preposition for each sentence. Sometimes, there is more than one answer. Also, prepositions are used in Idioms. These phrasal verbs must be memorized.

1. Fish swim _____ lakes _____ their friends.

2. Please read _____ least 4 pages.

3. Read the story _____ your homework.

4. And answer the questions _____ this book.

5. The book was made _____ Mr. Dahl.

6. The runner is running _____ the track.

7. He is _____ good shape.

8. He exercises _____ 3 hours every day.

9. Playing games _____ the internet is fun.

10. The test is _____. Please give me your tests and you can go home.

Prepositions 14

Fill in the blank
Write a proper preposition for each sentence. Sometimes, there is more than one answer. Also, prepositions are used in Idioms. These phrasal verbs must be memorized.

1.   This baseball game is boring. I'm going to turn _____ the TV.

2.   I like to read books _____ my bed.

3.   The rocket went _____ into the sky.

4.   The rocket is _____ a mission to the moon.

5.   Would you like to take a trip _____ the moon?

6.   The moon is far _____ us.

7.   _____ night, the sky is filled _____ stars.

8.   I can sing the song Twinkle Twinkle Little Star. I know the song _____ heart.

9.   Sadly, I am bad _____ singing.

10. This is the last sentence _____ this page.

Prepositions 15

Fill in the blank
Write a proper preposition for each sentence. Sometimes, there is more than one answer. Also, prepositions are used in Idioms. These phrasal verbs must be memorized.

1. Monkeys live _____ trees.

2. Potatoes grow _____ the ground.

3. My birthday is _____ March 16.

4. The man is sitting _____ a chair.

5. There is a light _____ our heads.

6. The letter B is _____ A and C.

7. They study _____ 9am.

8. They study _____ 9am _____ 4pm.

9. It's cold _____, so wear a hat.

10. We arrived _____ the airport early.

Picture
Practice

Let's start the picture practice part of the book by studying WHERE things are.
Look at the owls below. Where are they?

ON	IN	OVER	UNDER
FAR	NEAR	UP	DOWN

FRONT	BEHIND	BETWEEN	AROUND
OPPOSITE	THROUGH	FRIST	LAST

Picture Practice ②

1. Where are the apples?

2. Where is the lady?

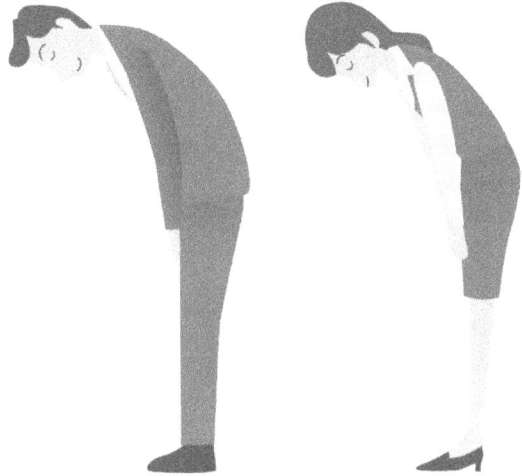

3. Where is the cat?

4. Where is the boy falling?

Picture Practice

(3)

1. What are they doing?

2. What is the lady doing?

3. What is she doing?

4. What is he doing?

5. What is he doing?

Picture Practice

1. The man is...

2. The woman is...

3. The robot is...

4. The boy is...

Picture Practice

(5)

1. What is he doing?

2. What are they doing?

3. What is the baby doing?

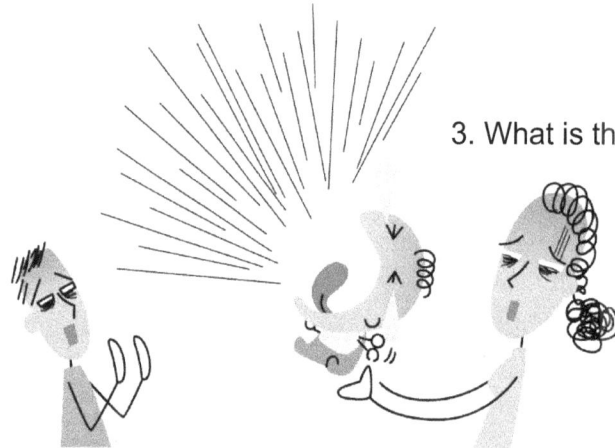

4. What are they doing?

5. What are the men doing?

Picture Practice

Finish the sentences.

1. The tree has many _____.

2. The girl has _____ in her hair.

3. The man has _____ in his knees.

4. The woman has a _____.

5. The students are having _____.

89

Picture Practice

What is happening in the story?

Write your story here:

1. _____
2. _____
3. _____
4. _____
5. _____
6. _____
7. _____

Picture Practice

What is happening in the story?

Write your story here:

1. _____
2. _____
3. _____
4. _____
5. _____
6. _____

Picture Practice

Finish the sentences.

1. What is the mom doing?

2. What are they doing, and who is taller?

3. Where is the man, and how is the weather?

4. What did the lion say to the elephant?

Picture Practice

1. What kind of house is this?

2. Who is stronger, you are Godzilla?

3. Where is the man, and how is the weather?

4. What wasn't the man doing?

5. How does the man smell?

The
Lie Game

Lie Game 1

Lie Game:
The sentences below are examples. You can use them to help you make sentences.

A - ANT, APPLE, AROUND

1. Ants are big.

2. Apples are delicious in autumn.

3. The moon flies around the sun.

☐
....

☐
....

☐
....

B - BUGS, BANANA, BEFORE

1. Some people eat bugs.

2. Bananas grow under trees.

3. Summer is before autumn.

☐
....

☐
....

☐
....

C - CAT, CARRY, CLOSE TO

1. Cats can climb trees.

2. Ants can't carry heavy things.

3. Japan is close to Korea.

☐
....

☐
....

☐
....

Lie Game 2

D - DON'T, DRAGON, DIRTY

1. Many students don't like homework.
2. Dragons are real.
3. Dirty people smell bad.

☐
_____

☐
_____

☐
_____

E - EAR, EARLY, EAT

1. People have 3 ears.
2. Old people usually wake up early.
3. Birds eat bugs.

☐
_____

☐
_____

☐
_____

F - FRIDAY, FEEL, FLY

1. Friday is after Saturday.
2. People feel cold in winter.
3. Chickens can't fly.

☐
_____

☐
_____

☐
_____

Lie Game 3

G - GO, GIRLS, GARBAGE

1. People like to go swimming in summer.
2. Girls usually have longer hair than boys.
3. Garbage smells good in summer.

   ☐

   ☐

   ☐

H - HAPPY, HAVE, HAIR

1. Students feel happy on holidays.
2. Students have to study hard.
3. All people have hair on their heads.

   ☐

   ☐

   ☐

I - INTERESTED, INTO, IGLOO

1. Doctors are interested in helping people.
2. Sometimes people jump into the sun.
3. Igloos are made of snow.

   ☐

   ☐

   ☐

Lie Game 4

J - JAM, JUMP, JACKET

1. Jam is made of chocolate.
2. Frogs can jump far.
3. Jackets are important in winter.

☐
....

☐
....

☐
....

K - KIWI, KIND, KOALA

1. Kiwis are a kind of fruit.
2. Students like kind teachers.
3. Koalas can run fast.

☐
....

☐
....

☐
....

L - LEMON, LIKE, LOUD

1. Lemons are sour.
2. Giraffes like to eat leaves.
3. Teachers like loud and noisy students.

☐
....

☐
....

☐
....

Lie Game 5

M - MONKEY, MAKE, MORE

1. Monkeys sometimes fall out of trees.
2. Bakers make clothes.
3. There are more people in China than in India.

☐

☐

☐

N - NO, NEVER, NEW

1. No people can fly.
2. Penguins never swim in winter.
3. New cars are shiny.

☐

☐

☐

O - OCTOPUS, ORANGE, ON

1. An octopus has 7 legs.
2. Oranges grow on trees.
3. People turn on lights at night.

☐

☐

☐

Lie Game 6

P - PUT, PEAR, PAPER

1. People put on pajamas in the morning.
2. Pears look like apples.
3. Paper is made from wood.

☐

☐

☐

Q - QUESTION, QUIET, BANQUET

1. Teachers like to ask questions to students.
2. Libraries aren't very quiet.
3. People eat food at banquets.

☐

☐

☐

R - RUN, ROUND, RHINO

1. Cheetahs run fast.
2. Pizza is round.
3. Rhinos don't have horns.

☐

☐

☐

Lie Game 7

S - SEVEN, SALT, SIT

1. There are seven days in a week.
2. People put salt in coffee.
3. People sit on benches in parks.

   ☐

   ☐

   ☐

T - TENNIS, TOMORROW, TABLE

1. Tennis is a sport.
2. Today is Monday. Tomorrow is Sunday.
3. Students need tables for studying.

   ☐

   ☐

   ☐

U - UMBRELLA, UNDER, UP

1. Umbrellas are good on windy days.
2. Clouds fly under the moon.
3. Old people usually wake up early.

   ☐

   ☐

   ☐

Lie Game 8

Lie Game:
The sentences below are examples. You can use them to help you make sentences.

V - VERY, VACATION, HEAVY

1. Gold is very heavy.
2. Everybody likes vacations.
3. Chickens are heavier than elephants.

☐ ....

☐ ....

☐ ....

W - WATERMELON, WEAK, TOWER

1. Watermelons have many seeds.
2. Lions are weak animals.
3. Towers are high buildings.

☐ ....

☐ ....

☐ ....

X, Y, Z - EXIT, YELLOW, ZEBRA

1. All buildings have exits.
2. Lemons are yellow and very sour.
3. Zebras look like pigs.

☐ ....

☐ ....

☐ ....

Making Perfect Questions

MPQ 1

For each sentence, write a question that answers it. For example, if the sentence is "I brush my teeth 3 times a day", the question could be "How often do you brush your teeth?" Many questions can be used for each sentence.

1. I'm 15 years old.

2. It's on the table.

3. I think it's a cat.

4. Yes, I can.

5. Tomorrow.

6. I have 1 sister.

7. I live in Tokyo.

8. It's 080-4500-1234.

9. I eat fruit every day.

10. He's my dad.

MPQ 2

For each sentence, write a question that answers it.

1. He is a doctor.

_____

2. He was born in Canada.

_____

3. No, I don't.

_____

4. China.

_____

5. I went to school.

_____

6. The test is next week.

_____

7. In the sky.

_____

8. One time a week.

_____

9. It was $5.

_____

10. Blue.

_____

MPQ 3

For each sentence, write a question that answers it.

1. I like the brown one.

2. It's mine.

3. Yes, I will.

4. In my mouth.

5. My dog's name is Wufwuf.

6. Your feet.

7. In the morning.

8. I got here at 9am.

9. Last week was my birthday.

10. In March.

MPQ 4

For each sentence, write a question that answers it.

1. F-E-B-R-U-A-R-Y

2. I'm fine thank you. And you?

3. I bought a pencil.

4. No, I haven't.

5. I think it's Russia.

6. I like apples.

7. I have only 1.

8. I came here by car.

9. I sleep 6 hours every night.

10. 10.

MPQ 5

For each sentence, write a question that answers it.

1. Because it's raining.

_____

2. I want to watch a movie.

_____

3. In France.

_____

4. Yes, I did.

_____

5. He is sleeping.

_____

6. My teacher.

_____

7. It looks like a bug.

_____

8. Maybe next summer.

_____

9. It's next to the park.

_____

10. Never.

_____

Making Perfect Sentences

MPS 1

Write a sentence using each word.

cat	
am	
of	
and	
ant	
to	
in	
head	
have	
ear	

MPS 2

Write a sentence using each word.

that	
finger	
they	
I	
with	
not	
on	
dad	
at	
by	

MPS 3

Write a sentence using each word.

this	
we	
yellow	
door	
but	
from	
or	
one	
window	
all	

MPS 4

will	
hair	
say	
make	
can	
more	
if	
no	
man	
out	

MPS 5

Write a sentence using each word.

so	
time	
up	
go	
about	
car	
into	
could	
only	
new	

MPS 6

year	
some	
take	
come	
TV	
know	
see	
use	
get	
like	

MPS 7

first	
any	
work	
now	
March	
give	
sky	
think	
monkey	
find	

MPS 8

Write a sentence using each word.

day	
after	
mom	
pizza	
little	
before	
great	
back	
long	
boy	

MPS 9

Write a sentence using each word.

well	
bear	
down	
because	
good	
feel	
high	
too	
bed	
wood	

MPS 10

Write a sentence using each word.

very	
still	
hand	
old	
chair	
tell	
write	
bug	
here	
horse	

MPS 11

Write a sentence using each word.

boat	
jam	
need	
call	
under	
lunch	
right	
move	
school	
never	

MPS 12

Write a sentence using each word.

same	
table	
my	
leave	
might	
want	
off	
few	
small	
ask	

MPS 13

Write a sentence using each word.

late	
ham	
large	
feet	
open	
sing	
heavy	
eye	
run	
keep	

MPS 14

play	
early	
help	
flower	
chicken	
fly	
remember	
later	
pretty	
alligator	

MPS 15

car	
spider	
Monday	
point	
touch	
start	
end	
moon	
bag	
her	

MPS 16

Write a sentence using each word.

drink	
Japan	
carry	
use	
five	
tree	
desk	
climb	
angry	
sad	

Writing: Short Stories

Short Story 1

THE FRIENDLY TREE

PICTURE

Short Story 2

THE HUNGRY CAT

PICTURE

Short Story 3

A RAINY DAY

PICTURE

Short Story 4

THE DIRTY BROTHER

PICTURE

Short Story 5

THE TALKING SHOES

PICTURE

Short Story 6

THE BABY DINOSAUR

PICTURE

Short Story 7

BOO! ARE YOU SCARED?

PICTURE

Short Story 8

GOODBYE MR. CLOUD

PICTURE

Short Story 9

THE SAILBOAT

PICTURE

Short Story 10

GRIPPALI THE CHIMPANZEE

PICTURE

Appendix

LIST OF PREPOSITIONS

Prepositions are words that tells us about where something is, or when something happens. They are always used to talk about nouns, like **on** TV, **in** my hand, or **above** my head. Here is a list of common prepositions:

aboard	about	above	across	After	against
ahead of	all over	along	among	Apart	around
as	At	away	away from	Back	before
behind	below	beneath	between	beyond	by
close by	close to	despite	down	during	except
for	forward	from	in	in between	in front of
inside	into	like	near	next to	of
off	on	on top of	opposite	outside	onto
over	out	out of	round	Past	since
through	to	toward	towards	under	until
upon	up	with	within	without	

OSASCNM – THE ORDER OF ADJECTIVES

In English, you must use adjectives in the certain order in a sentence. You must not mix up the order of the adjectives. It is one of English grammar rules.

If you can remember OSASCNM, then you will know the order of adjectives.

O = Opinion, **S** = Size, **A** = Age, **S** = Shape, **C** = Colour, **N** = Nationality, **M** = Material

◎ I have a <u>nice</u>, <u>big</u>, <u>old</u>, <u>square</u>, <u>brown</u>, <u>Canadian</u>, <u>wooden</u> chair.
      O   S   A   S   C   N   M

× I have a <u>big</u>, <u>square</u>, <u>Canadian</u>, <u>old</u>, <u>brown</u>, <u>nice</u> <u>wooden</u> chair.
      S   S   N   A   C   O   M

LIST OF IRREGULAR VERBS

Infinitive	Simple Past	Past Participle
be	was/were	been
beat	beat	beaten
become	became	become
begin	began	begun
bet*	bet	bet
blow	blew	blown
break	broke	broken
bring	brought	brought
build	built	built
buy	bought	bought
catch	caught	caught
choose	chose	chosen
come	came	come
cost	cost	cost
cut	cut	cut
deal	dealt	dealt
do	did	done
draw	drew	drawn
drink	drank	drunk
drive	drove	driven
eat	ate	eaten
fall	fell	fallen
feed	fed	fed
feel	felt	felt

Infinitive	Simple Past	Past Participle
fight	fought	fought
find	found	found
fly	flew	flown
forget	forgot	forgotten
freeze	froze	frozen
get	got	got, gotten
give	gave	given
go	went	gone
grow	grew	grown
hang	hung	hung
have	had	had
hear	heard	heard
hide	hid	hidden
hit	hit	hit
hold	held	held
hurt	hurt	hurt
keep	kept	kept
know	knew	known
lead	led	led
leave	left	left
lend	lent	lent
let	let	let
light*	lit	lit
lose	lost	lost
make	made	made
mean	meant	meant
meet	met	met

Infinitive	Simple Past	Past Participle
pay	paid	paid
put	put	put
read	read	read
ride	rode	ridden
ring	rang	rung
rise	rose	risen
run	ran	run
say	said	said
see	saw	seen
sell	sold	sold
send	sent	sent
set	set	set
shake	shook	shaken
steal	stole	stolen
shine	shone	shone
shoot	shot	shot
shut	shut	shut
sing	sang	sung
sink	sank	sunk
sit	sat	sat
sleep	slept	slept
slide	slid	slid
speak	spoke	spoken
spend	spent	spent
stand	stood	stood
stick	stuck	stuck
swear	swore	sworn

Infinitive	Simple Past	Past Participle
sweep	swept	swept
swim	swam	swum
swing	swung	swung
take	took	taken
teach	taught	taught
tear	tore	torn
tell	told	told
think	thought	thought
throw	threw	thrown
understand	understood	understood
wake*	woke	woken
wear	wore	worn
win	won	won
write	wrote	written

155

www.ingramcontent.com/pod-product-compliance
Lightning Source LLC
Chambersburg PA
CBHW081426090426
42740CB00017B/3193